STAR SONGS

A Book of Inspired Astrology

Velma S

fenton Valley press

Storrs, Connecticut

Copyright 1987 by Velma Swann
First printing 1987

10   9   8   7   6   5   4   3   2   1

Published by

Fenton Valley Press
657 Chaffeeville Road
Storrs, Connecticut 06268
203-429-0710

We are a small publishing company dedicated to creating
lovingly crafted books that nourish the inner life.
Write to us if you would like to be notified
of our other publications, or use the
ordering information at the back
of this book.

Typeset by Advantage Graphics

Acid-free paper

Printed in the United States of America
by Bookcrafters, Inc., Chelsea, Michigan

International Standard Book Number: 0-9615149-8-1
Library of Congress Card Catalog Number: 87-80999

CONTENTS

PROLOGUE

A sacred thing
is the order
of the universe,
nothing left
to chance
or whim.
As a soul
travels through
each and every
sign,
it may be lazy
or slow,
even negative,
but it must return
over and over
until the potential
of each sign
is achieved.
When the full beauty
and glory
of all reincarnations
have been fulfilled,
the soul is free
to join
THE PLANE OF LOVE.

ARIES

March 21 - April 20

A sign of belief and courage and daring. A sign needing to lead others, even when they do not know the way themselves. A sign of impulsiveness and childlike joy and many small angers. Born in the cycle of time to jar others loose from the ruts of earth, to compel them to inquire and to go forward and achieve. Aries, the sons and daughters of Energy, keep the earth in motion.

STAR SONGS
FROM ARIES

I just wanted
to be
your knight
in shining armor.
I did not mean
to trample you
with
my horse's hooves.

LIKE a child
I offered you
my heart.
You hesitate.
Do you dare
to win
my love,
then
be afraid
of my fire?

DON'T
reach for me.
By myself
I will unravel
this cloth
of pain
you have made
of my life.
Then
by myself
I will knit
a new cloth
of bright, glowing colors.

SORRY,
I did not
see you.
I was too busy
listening
to the song
in my head
and following
the dream
in my heart.

TAURUS

April 21 - May 21

The sons and daughters of earth, a sign truly in harmony with the earth's vibrations. A sign of rock, slow and eternal, as deep-rooted to the earth as a cedar tree. A sign that can often see the wings of angels, but does not desire to fly with them. The pulls of earth, its beauty and its duties, are strong in this sign. Born in the cycle of time to show others the comfort and value of earthly things, to help stabilize those who are out of tune with earth's vibrations.

STAR SONGS
FROM TAURUS

LET me out
to the spirits
of wind and sky,
lest my soul
turn to stone.

I can not
sit here
when the rain
smells so good.
I must put on my coat
and go
to it.

TO *say*
that you
did not know
is not enough
for me now.

I am not
a gambler.
There are things
about you
that I do not trust
enough for forever,
and there are things
that I must let go
for you
that I do not know
if I can.

THIS moment
this day
is too heavy
for me.
I have to
lift myself out
and up
to the blue-green
of tomorrow
and remember
that this now
is just a space
in the vastness
of forever.

GEMINI

May 22 - June 21

A sign of thought on all levels, a mind that travels and flits around with great speed, a sign that seeks to take the fragments of life and form them into a whole. A sign that needs a strong base of security to operate from in order to function best. Born in the cycle of time as a transmitter. A soul that picks up information from all the vibrations around it, condenses it into a concrete knowledge and communicates it to other souls.

STAR SONGS
FROM GEMINI

I go
through life
lighting candles,
but others
keep snuffing them out.
That is why
I keep
plenty of matches.

BLESSED
are the
receivers,
for we must learn
to be
transmitters.

I have to
stop this clamor
inside my head.
I will
run
deep into
the silence
and maybe
I will find
God waiting there.

I was always
looking
for the light
at the end
of the tunnel,
never seeing
that the light
was all around.

*I feel
that if someone
runs hot and cold,
you better get out
of the creekbed.*

CANCER

June 22 - July 23

The lambs of life, complaining as they go gently through the pastures of earth. A sign needing comfort and peace, home and stability. A sign that yearns to tenderly protect others. Born in the cycle of time to be the guardians of earth. A sign that has a heavy responsibility to keep the bonds of family strong, to be a steady bulwark against the decadence of earth.

STAR SONGS
FROM CANCER

I wanted to do
so many things.
I planned
a home
with dotted curtains
and laughing children
and flowers everywhere.
I wanted to sit
on the porch
and grow old,
but I wanted
to do it
with you.

❧

MY harmony
is created
on the fine edge
of despair.

*THERE was a time
when we saw
the same truth
and I could
take your hand
and pull you
to the hearth.
But today
my face is
but a shadow
on the fringe
of your mind
and my words
are meaningless fragments
thrown to the great void
of space.*

SORROW
brought my soul
near the surface,
so the sunlight
of God
could reach it better.

I must keep
my roots strong
and my branches
limber in the wind,
until I can
pass over
into the warm climate
of God.

LEO

July 24 - August 23

True children of the gods, a sign of pride, laughter, friends and family, quick tempers and easy forgiveness. A sign that can never be happy without much giving and receiving of love. Born in the cycle of time to show others the true meaning of brotherhood and charity. A sign of fire, that gives warmth to a cold earth.

STAR SONGS
FROM LEO

STRONG Leo,
who bluffs his way
through life
and wins.
Tender Leo,
who seeks
to protect
and refuses
to stand aside
for Fate.
Brave Leo,
who dares
to fight
and loses
because of
too much love.

*WHATEVER else
my life
has been,
I have always
felt
the melody
and the energy
and the beat
of every moment
on earth.*

*HEY, ho!
I'm off
to purchase
a sword
and a horse
so as to
rescue myself.*

*I will not
let love
bend and break
me again.
I am
going away
to fly
with my own wings.
If love wants me,
he can
search me out.*

VIRGO

August 24 - September 23

The workers of earth, a sign with a need to serve others and bring order to the life about them. A conservative sign of logic and harmony. Without these, the sign often goes into deep depression. A sign that seeks love through giving. Born in the cycle of time to give a much-needed balance to earth.

STAR SONGS
FROM VIRGO

IF you
had searched
through stones
long enough,
you would have known
that I am
a gem.

WHY do
great changes
in my life
always seem
to sneak up
on me?

I just can not
bend
and sniff a daisy
without worrying
that there may be
a bee inside.

HE was
a torch
to your soul,
but I am
the bread of life.

YOU *asked me*
to run
with you
through
the green joy
of Spring,
but I
could not
even see Spring.

I wish that
I had
put my face
to the wind,
instead of
watching
for thorns
on the ground.

LIBRA

September 24 - October 23

A sign of mood swings, due to a need to create a balance on every level. A sign that feels the allure of challenge and adventure, but sees too clearly the dangers. In striving to blend opposing factors in their beings and find a compromise, Libras often create great works of art, music or literature. Born in the cycle of time to encourage positive outlets for chaos, to give a beauty and dignity to earth.

STAR SONGS
FROM LIBRA

I want
a gentle love
with deep roots,
strong enough
to shelter me
from life's storms.

I will lie back
on my silken cushions
and pretend
they are clouds.
I hear the music
and I hear you
telling me your dreams . . .
but did you remember
to turn out
the lights,
put out the cat
and pay
the phone bill?

WISH I *was*
a pretty little girl.
I'd pick a flower,
put it in my hair,
play in the sunlight
and laugh at the night.
I'd touch and smell and see
and cry on my mamma's knee.
But pretty little girls
grow up
to watch flowers wilt
and see shadows
in the sunlight,
fear
in the night.
Pretty little girls
grow up to be
too big
for their mamma's knee.

SOMETIMES I *can soar*
above the sweat
and sordidness
of earth.
Sometimes . . .
I can not.

DEAL gently
with me,
for a weight
crushes my heart
and my soul
is caught
halfway between
heaven and earth.

THIS home,
my family
are life to me,
but sometimes
deep in the night
I hear a melody
from lifetimes past
and there are days
I see
beyond the sun
to the Place of Light,
and while I serve and love
there grows
a restlessness
in me.

SCORPIO

October 24 - November 22

Children of shadows and moonbeams. A paradox, a sign of power and great strength, yet deep tenderness. A sign of wisdom combined with dangerous emotion. A sign of fierce intensity and still deep waters. Born in the cycle of time to endure and overcome, an inspiration for weaker signs. A sign that is destined to seek out many strange paths, not realizing that they are in a constant quest for God.

STAR SONGS
FROM SCORPIO

I will light a fire
in your soul,
initiate you
to the mysteries,
make what is ugly in you
beautiful
and take you
to the heights of ecstasy.
But I am no haven.
I will entwine your roots
so tightly
they must struggle
for their very air.
I will advance, flow,
then brutally retreat
and fling you to the pits.
With me you will have
perfection of union
and unearthly tendresse
or you will flee
clothed only
in the rags
of your shredded soul.

WATCHING *snowflakes*
from my window,
I saw you
alone on the sidewalk
gazing up at me.
When you
pushed me down,
you should have known
what I would do
when
I got back up.

TENSE . . .
like a panther . . .
standing
on the raw edge
of panic.

THE music
sifts in
and wraps itself
around my pain
and it grows
like a living thing,
and the memories
file through
my head
like scenes
from a movie reel.
Ah, what was
it all for
anyway?

REPEAT performance:
Tomorrow
I will get up
and move
the whole
damn mountain!
But tonight . . .
let me have
my despair.

*I will laugh
and play
and carry
this burden
of pain.
I will live
and strive
and follow
the destiny
that I must
and never
even speak
your name.
But I will
love you
still
on the day
that I die.*

JUST yesterday
I was giving up,
but the power
descended on me
and set me free.

SAGITTARIUS

November 23 - December 21

A sign blessed with sweetness of heart. A sign of popularity and friendship. A sign with a desire to communicate and spread good cheer. A sign of adventure and the desire to travel. Born in the cycle of time to garner insight, to learn to let go of the superficial, and to seek out the inborn vision within their deeper being.

STAR SONGS
FROM SAGITTARIUS

IT *is a gift*
of the Fates,
that I never
meet a stranger.
The people
always
know me.

YES, *I guess that*
I did feel
that way . . .
the memory brings
a sweet sadness.
But . . .
that was
yesterday!

WHAT is failure
to me
when a Spring breeze
is playing
with my hair!

WATCHING the others
run through
the fire,
I wait my turn
calmly,
knowing
at the final minute
Fate will
throw me
an asbestos coat.

I said,
"God knows
and He understands."
They said,
"God knows
but He is stunned!"

CAPRICORN

December 22 - January 20

A sign at war with itself. A mental sign with a need to explore and experiment and collect, a naturally eccentric sign. Yet a cautious sign that has a deeper need to be proper and sophisticated and upstanding, a sign with a fear of being different. Born in the cycle of time to seek the quiet byways in order to meditate and come to terms with the values in life. Born to bring a higher intellect to earth.

STAR SONGS
FROM CAPRICORN

I need
to go slowly,
take the time
to read
the vast amount
of fine print
between
the lines.

I keep searching
for steel
and
finding plastic.

I can not
turn back.
Now I must
cross this
bridge of pain.
I have stood
at the water's edge
too long.

CAR and the highway
slicing through
the night.
Too much sorrow
hidden
in the backrooms
of my mind.
Tonight
the world
is too big
for me.

I am like
a fine-paged book,
containing
wondrous things,
that has not
been opened yet.

ENCLOSED
in the silence
of loneliness,
my soul
grew.

AQUARIUS
January 21 - February 19

A sign of brilliance and ideas, a sign with a need to enlighten and teach. A sign that accepts life and other people naturally, an open sign with few closed doors. A noble sign with a great need to share. Born in the cycle of time to learn to overcome their own confusion and procrastination, in order that they may clear the way for others.

STAR SONGS
FROM AQUARIUS

I tried
to shape my soul
into the mold
of the masses
and ended up
lopsided!

COME
and rest yourself
at my hearth.
Have no fear,
I will not
lock the door.

YES, I see
little pieces
of God
in everyone
I meet,
but pieces
are not enough
for me.

I'M fixing
to get up
and set the world
on fire . . .
any minute now.

I thought
the road
was hot steel,
but when
I looked back
I saw
it was solid gold.

PISCES

February 20 - March 20

The children of angels, living in a haze of clouds and sunbeams. A sign desperately needing to be understood. A passive sign that often retreats from harshness, either physical or emotional. A sign that will seek gratification in many ways, but will only find happiness in loving and giving to others. Born in the cycle of time to soften the rough edges of life, to give romanticism and dreams to a weary earth.

STAR SONGS
FROM PISCES

DO not awaken me
from my dreams,
for
they are better
than life.

I will
find a way
to live
in truth.
I will blind my eyes
and close my ears
and seek
the soul.

FROM too many wounds
my heart bleeds,
but somewhere
there is a velvet place
for me,
blue-green
and sprinkled
with stardust.
I know 'tis there;
sometimes a bit
of fairy glitter
caught on the wind
blows from there to me.

GIVE me today
to understand
your words
of yesterday.

THE color and glitter
I see beyond
beckon me.
Where,
oh where,
are my fairy wings?

EPILOGUE

Our stars
can light the way,
a map
through the tangle
of our lives,
but we alone
must make the journey.

STAR SIGNS OF SPECIAL PEOPLE

Sign	Name	Birthday
ARIES		
TAURUS		
GEMINI		

CANCER

59

LEO

VIRGO

LIBRA

SCORPIO

SAGITTARIUS

CAPRICORN

AQUARIUS

PISCES

WELL-LOVED SPIRITUAL BOOKS
from Fenton Valley Press

Fenton Valley Press is dedicated to creating beautiful inspirational books for people of all spiritual paths and all ages. If you liked *Star Songs*, you may also like these special books:

Heart of Gold: The Light Within Life, by Mary Pat Fisher. 25 uplifting passages from a high, clear place. A cherished bedside devotional, catalyst for personal meditations, and source of strength and inspiration during difficult times.

> 72 pages, soft cover, decorated with illuminated capitals and antique ornaments. $6.00.

Beneath the Snow, by Mark Dix. A fast-moving fantasy adventure in which a sensitive boy discovers his inner strength in a hidden wilderness, where wolves, a half-wild girl, and a master of camouflage become his teachers.

> 112 pages, soft cover, illustrated with Native American motifs and real snow crystals. $8.95.

Remember the Light, by Mary Pat Fisher. The moving and inspiring picture story of a young being of light who is sent to the land of darkness to remind the people of their love and beauty. Deeply loved by all ages.

> 32 pages, soft cover, illustrated with 17 delicate drawings. $4.50.

Available at your bookstore or from Fenton Valley Press. When ordering, please add $1.00 for Book Rate postage for the first book and 50¢ for each additional book. Connecticut residents please add 7½% sales tax. Thank you for sharing these special books.

Fenton Valley Press, 657 Chaffeeville Road, Storrs, CT 06268
Phone 203-429-0710

COLOPHON

Star Songs is typeset in Goudy Oldstyle and decorated with early-twentieth-century Italian ornaments selected from the Dover Pictorial Archives (*Treasury of Book Ornament and Decoration* and *Treasury of Art Nouveau Design and Ornament*). The recurring starburst motif is taken from a Roman entablature found in Albano near Rome, recorded by Alexander Speltz in *The Styles of Ornament*, 1904.